MAKEPOVERTYHISTORY

How You Can Help Defeat World Poverty
in Seven Easy Steps

by Geraldine Bedell

PENGUIN BOOKS

PENGUIN BOOKS

Published by the Penguin Group
Penguin Books Ltd, 80 Strand, London WC2R 0RL, England
Penguin Group (USA) Inc., 375 Hudson Street, New York, New York 10014, USA
Penguin Group (Canada), 10 Eglinton Avenue East, Suite 700, Toronto, Ontario, Canada M4P 2Y3
(a division of Pearson Penguin Canada Inc.)
Penguin Ireland, 25 St Stephen's Green, Dublin 2, Ireland
(a division of Penguin Books Ltd)
Penguin Group (Australia), 250 Camberwell Road, Camberwell, Victoria 3124, Australia
(a division of Pearson Australia Group Pty Ltd)
Penguin Books India Pvt Ltd, 11 Community Centre,
Panchsheel Park, New Delhi – 110 017, India
Penguin Group (NZ), cnr Airborne and Rosedale Roads, Albany, Auckland 1310, New Zealand
(a division of Pearson New Zealand Ltd)
Penguin Books (South Africa) (Pty) Ltd, 24 Sturdee Avenue, Rosebank, Johannesburg 2196, South Africa

Penguin Books Ltd, Registered Offices: 80 Strand, London WC2R 0RL, England

www.penguin.com

Published 2005

7

Copyright © Make Poverty History, 2005

Special thanks to parallel.net Ltd mailing house for waiving
their normal fee and packaging and posting

The moral right of the copyright holder has been asserted

Set in Frutiger
Printed in England by Clays Ltd, St Ives plc

'It is from the numberless diverse acts of courage and belief that human history is shaped. Each time a man stands up for an ideal, or acts to improve the lot of others, or strikes out against injustice, he sends a tiny ripple of hope, and crossing each other from a million different centres of energy and daring, those ripples build a current which can sweep down the mightiest walls of oppression or resistance.'

Senator Robert Kennedy

'To stay quiet is as political an act as speaking out.'

Arundhati Roy, author and Indian activist

'It is not the kings and generals who make history, but the masses of the people.'

Nelson Mandela

Thanks and acknowledgements

The Make Poverty History coalition would like to thank Geraldine Bedell, who wrote this book on our behalf, for doing such a brilliant job in a very short space of time. And the *Observer*, who gave her the time to write it.

We would also like to thank Penguin Books, who generously agreed to publish the book on a non-profit basis, Guy Hughes for co-ordination and research, Marcus Tomlinson and Rankin for taking the photographs that appear on the inside covers, and the many members of Make Poverty History who contributed time and resources to make the book possible.

Finally we would thank all the people in Britain and around the world who have responded to our call to take action and are supporting our campaigning to Make Poverty History in 2005.

Contents

Preface

Take a moment to complete this quiz.

What kind of person are you?

 Do you think it's wrong that 50,000 people die of poverty every day?

 Do you think it's wrong that a child dies of poverty every 3 seconds?

 Do you think it's strange and perplexing that people don't talk about this on buses and in pubs, at school and college and work; that no one says 'Have you heard? 18 million people will die this year unnecessarily – that's millions more than the population of London'?

 Do you find the issues confusing? Do you suspect you don't quite understand, for example, how trade policies make poor countries poorer?

 Would you like to do something about this but haven't got the faintest idea what?

 Are you sure it's right to be upset about this, but still unsure what to answer when people say, 'But they're all corrupt anyway,' or 'Suppose we gave enough aid to save Africa's children. Wouldn't there be a population explosion and a lot more hungry adults'?

If you answered 'yes' to all of these questions, or even some of them, then you are a normal person.

And this book is for you. It's a self-help guide to defeating poverty.

All you have to do is follow the seven steps. It's surprisingly easy and certainly takes a lot less willpower than other self-help regimes – to help you give up smoking, say, or to lose weight. And ending extreme poverty, disease and despair – that's something everyone can agree on. Unlike giving up chocolate.

So we should do it. Each chapter is about a separate subject – and each chapter ends with a 'to do' list. Do them – and you really could make a difference.

Ending poverty is not about charity, it's about justice.

The changes we need aren't monstrous or unimaginable. But they will require everyone to do something this year.

Bono has speculated that our generation will be remembered for three things – the internet, the war on terror, and our attitude to the poor: whether we end extreme, 'stupid' poverty once and for all. History, he has said,

'will be our judge, but what's written is up to us. Who we are, who we've been, what we want to be remembered for. We can't say our generation didn't know how to do it. We can't say our generation couldn't afford to do it. And we can't say our generation didn't have reason to do it.'

This little book is to help you make us the generation that did it.

Step 1

Make a Difference with Make Poverty History

You think poverty is just too complicated and *big*? Can't see how you can possibly influence world leaders, international bankers, European trade policy when you have enough trouble influencing your mum, your boy/girlfriend, your children, your wife, yourself?

Well, changing the world just got easier.

Make Poverty History is your way of getting your voice heard – a unique alliance of charities, trade unions, campaigning organizations, faith communities and celebrities that have banded together to make 2005 the year that things start to look different.

More than 400 UK organizations are involved in Make Poverty History, and Make Poverty History is itself part of a wider coalition of groups from sixty-one countries on every continent, united by the snappy title of The Global Call To Action Against Poverty. From Southampton to Stirling, from Senegal to Sri Lanka, people have chosen this year as the year they're picking a fight with the root causes of extreme poverty.

PS. You can check what's happening around the world at: www.whiteband.org

In 2005, more than ever, you're not on your own in this. **You're with**

Nelson Mandela:

' Massive poverty and obscene inequality are such terrible scourges of our times – times in which the world boasts breathtaking advances in science, technology, industry and wealth accumulation – that they have to rank alongside slavery and apartheid as social evils.

The Global Call To Action Against Poverty can take its place as a public movement alongside the movement to abolish slavery and the international solidarity against apartheid.

I can never thank the people of Britain enough for their support through those days of the struggle against apartheid. Many stood in solidarity with us, just a few yards from this spot. Through your will and passion, you assisted in consigning that evil system for ever to history.

But in this new century, many of the world's poorest countries remain imprisoned, enslaved and in chains. They are trapped in the prison of poverty. It is time to set them free.

Like slavery and apartheid, poverty is not natural. It is man-made and it can be overcome and eradicated by the actions of human beings. '

Trafalgar Square, 3 February 2005

So why is now the moment for you to do something?

It's about time, frankly, but 2005 also happens to be an unusual year, a unique opportunity.

This is the year that Britain chairs the G8 (Group of Eight), the club of rich nations (Britain, France, Germany, Japan, Italy, the USA, Canada and Russia) whose leaders will meet at Gleneagles in Scotland on July 6–8. For the first time ever, poverty and development are at the top of the agenda.

Britain also takes over the presidency of the EU, which means an opportunity to change the trade rules.

And 2005 marks the twentieth anniversary of Live Aid, a rare moment when the entire world seemed to come together with a common purpose. Yet in the two decades since, Africa has got poorer.

There's *another* important meeting in December – this time of the World Trade Organization, in Hong Kong.

And crucially, it's five years since the world made the Millennium Promise, when every single country committed to a timetable to halve extreme poverty by 2015. These were real promises, which poor countries took extremely seriously. But if radical progress is not made this year, then the rich countries will definitely fail to meet them, and it could be decades until these issues come to the forefront again.

These promises are being reviewed at a meeting in September in New York at the United Nations Millennium Development Goals Summit.

For the poorest people, 2005 is a make or break year.

So imagine you're stuck in a lift with the

Prime Minister

What are you going to say to him?

(a) *'How are the wife and kids?'*
(b) *Er...nothing.*
(c) *'There is a solution to world poverty, and it requires three things:*

1. **Trade justice** – "Why should we demand poor countries give up protecting their own businesses? We won't give up protecting ours!"

2. **More and better aid** – "Why don't we give the 0.7% of national income in aid that we promised thirty-five years ago?"

3. **Drop the debt** – "Why are some poor countries still spending more on debt repayments than on the most basic needs of their own people?"

'Thanks for listening. Now, please, could you do something about it?

'I believe this is the ground floor.'

This year, why not go for (c). You can ask about the wife and kids next year.

The To Do List: 1

**Start influencing world events now.
Go to the Make Poverty History website at
www.makepovertyhistory.org
and click on 'Join us now'.**

Once you've signed up, Make Poverty History will
e-mail you, keeping you up to date about how you
can be part of bringing an end to poverty.
The more people sign up and support Make Poverty
History's goals, the more politicians will know that this
is the year they have to take action.

Time taken: 3 minutes.
Cost: none.

And if you're not on e-mail, then write to us at
Make Poverty History, c/o BOND, Regent's Wharf,
8 All Saints St, London N1 9RL.

Time taken: 5 minutes.
Cost: the price of a stamp.

**Plus: E-mail the website address to a couple
of friends.**

It's not half as painful as dieting – and imagine that
the Prime Minister did something as a result of your
conversation in the lift. How would you feel? If
enough people join up this year and make their
feelings known – that's how you will feel by this
Christmas.

Step 2

Become Part of History

It's worth getting involved with Make Poverty History because we *know* that campaigning works. Here are a few examples which show that the world can really be changed.

The Anti-Slavery Movement

At the end of the eighteenth century, well over three-quarters of the people alive were in bondage, subject to various forms of slavery and serfdom. Yet even more astonishing than the extent of slavery was the speed with which it died. By the end of the following century, keeping slaves was officially outlawed almost everywhere. The anti-slavery movement had achieved its goal in little more than one lifetime.

This happened because former slaves toured Britain, talking about life on the plantations and slave ships, while anti-slavery activists demonstrated handcuffs, shackles and thumbscrews. The campaigners used the postal services, newspapers, books and pamphlets. They held meetings. They were powered by a belief that human beings had the capacity to care about others, and they were right: the campaign in Britain was something the world had never seen before – the first time a large number of people became outraged over someone else's rights. What's more, they were the rights of another people, of another colour, on another continent.

Within a few years, more than 300,000 Britons were refusing to eat slave-grown sugar. An abolition committee existed in every major town or city. Parliament was flooded with petitions: the one from Edinburgh stretched the length of the Commons' floor; 20,000 people signed in Manchester, nearly one-third of the population. In smaller towns, petitions bore the signatures of every literate inhabitant. More people signed petitions than were eligible to vote. People got involved who had never been involved in politics before, especially women.

Anti-slavery was the first grass-roots human rights campaign. And it worked. Within a few years the Home Secretary was adopting the language of the campaigners, saying he was in favour of abolition.

The abolition of slavery is estimated to have cost the British people 1.8% of their annual income – many times more than we give in aid today. No one complained. Most of the people protesting had never seen a slave. Yet in our day, everyone has seen the devastation caused by poverty on our TV screens.

The Anti-Apartheid Campaign

The anti-apartheid campaign began in 1959 with an economic boycott of South African potatoes and fruit and quickly turned into a much wider movement for the complete dismantling of the apartheid South African regime, which suppressed the non-white majority. It was the first time that groups of local activists, trade unions and local authorities had direct impact on the UN and the Commonwealth; and it changed British foreign policy.

Anti-apartheid was always a mass movement, with early meetings addressed by politicians from all sides. Supporters included people of faith and no faith, professionals, trade unionists and the unemployed, black and ethnic groups and women's organizations.

Tactics were calculated to make an impact: demonstrations against the Springbok cricket tour in 1970, after which South Africa was eventually expelled from nearly every sporting federation; the vigil outside South Africa House in Trafalgar Square; the Wembley concert in 1988 on the eve of Nelson Mandela's seventieth birthday, which was seen on television by a billion people in sixty countries. By the mid-1980s, business was finally listening: Barclays Bank and others began selling off their South African subsidiaries.

For thirty-five years, hundreds of thousands of British people joined anti-apartheid campaigns, signed petitions, refused to buy South African produce, went to concerts, demonstrated, lobbied international institutions, kept a vigil outside South Africa House. By explaining what apartheid really meant, the campaign ensured there was no longer any doubt in people's minds that it was evil.

In the end, there was almost no one left to defend South Africa; and, isolated, it had no future. On 11 February 1990 Nelson Mandela was released from prison. Four years later South Africa held its first free general election and he was inaugurated as President.

Jubilee 2000 –
the Drop the Debt Campaign

Starting with a small group of activists, Jubilee 2000 mobilized 24 million people internationally over five years behind the slogan 'Drop the Debt' – a demand to cancel the unpayable debts of the poorest countries by 2000.

In common with the campaigns above, Jubilee 2000 had a broadly based membership, taking in black refugee groups, the Mothers' Union and the British Medical Association. Staff and volunteers of pressure groups, charities and associations combined with individuals who weren't part of any group. And, like the campaigners above, the supporters of Jubilee 2000 deployed a range of tactics: distributing leaflets, writing articles, organizing meetings, staffing stalls, chaining themselves to railings.

On 16 May 1998, 70,000 people demonstrated in Birmingham, the planned venue for the G7, the meeting of the finance ministers of the world's richest countries. A decision had belatedly been taken to move the G7 elsewhere, to keep the leaders away from the demonstrators, but by early afternoon it was clear that this had been a strategic error. Prime Minister Tony Blair announced that he was flying back from the country-house meeting early: could he meet representatives of Jubilee 2000?

When 24 million people sign a petition, politicians have to sit up and take notice. In 1999, at the Cologne G8 summit, world leaders agreed to cancel $100 billion of debts owed by the poorest countries.

Not so amusing facts . . .

- World trade has increased tenfold since 1970, and more food is produced than ever before, yet the number of people going hungry in Africa has doubled. More than 800 million people go hungry every day. At current rates of progress, it would take 130 years to rid the world of hunger.

- More than 1 billion people lack access to safe drinking water.

- The three richest people in the world control more wealth than all 600 million people in the world's poorest countries.

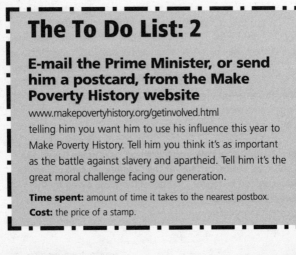

The To Do List: 2

E-mail the Prime Minister, or send him a postcard, from the Make Poverty History website

www.makepovertyhistory.org/getinvolved.html

telling him you want him to use his influence this year to Make Poverty History. Tell him you think it's as important as the battle against slavery and apartheid. Tell him it's the great moral challenge facing our generation.

Time spent: amount of time it takes to the nearest postbox.
Cost: the price of a stamp.

'I'd love you, as you read this, to ask yourself "What can I do this year?" – and then do it. Everyone: young, old, rich, poor, trade unionist, businessman, diplomat, Conservative, Labour, Liberal, Green, churchgoer, concertgoer, teacher, writer, actor. I beg you, don't see this moment, this opportunity for change, and then waste the opportunity.'

Richard Curtis, scriptwriter, co-founder of Comic Relief, January 2005

Read on to find out exactly what you're asking for…

Step 3

Insist on More and Better Aid

Think, for a second, what your kitchen and bathroom might look like if you lived on less than 65p a day.

You wouldn't have a bathroom. Or a kitchen. You'd be lucky if the nearest source of water was clean, if it didn't involve a walk. You'd be unusual if you could afford enough food, let alone the fuel to cook it.

CURRENTLY 1 BILLION PEOPLE, ONE IN SIX OF THE WORLD'S POPULATION, LIVE ON LESS THAN 65P A DAY.

The case for more aid isn't difficult to understand. How many women do you know who have died from pregnancy or in childbirth? Worldwide, a woman dies every minute from complications associated with having a baby; 99% of these deaths are in the developing world. If it almost never happens here, it should almost never happen anywhere.

How many children do you know who have died from drinking water? In the developing world, a child dies every fifteen seconds from water-related diseases. These deaths are entirely preventable.

Basic healthcare would save the lives of millions. A doubling of the aid budget to $100 billion a year would help achieve this and allow the world to make serious progress towards the Millennium Development Goals, listed on page 25.

So why isn't it happening? Is it that the world simply can't afford it?

Well, if you piled the extra $50 billion the developing world needs, it would be very high indeed – as high as a space shuttle orbiting the earth, in fact. It is a lot of money. But . . . the truth is that as the rich world has got richer, it has got less, not more, generous. Rich countries give the poor the equivalent of a price of a cup of coffee a week from each of their citizens – half as much, as a proportion of income, as they did in the 1960s.

In 1970, rich nations agreed to spend 0.7% of their national incomes on development aid. Thirty-five years later, the world is still waiting for it to happen.

Doubling aid is not a new idea – it is what we promised years and years ago and what we have been consistently drifting away from for years and years.

The good news is that Britain is starting to wake up: we have committed to raising the percentage of Britain's national income spent on aid to 0.47% by 2008. But we need to remember that in 1979 we already spent more than that – 0.51% – and that only five of the twenty-two major donors have achieved the target.

This pattern is repeated across the rich world. That's a dismal sign of how, despite all the passion of Live Aid, the governments of the rich world haven't become more generous.

Britain's new pledge will at least provide an extra $1.5 billion of aid by 2008. And if growth continues at that rate, we will meet the 0.7% goal by 2013. In other words, the extra money can be found.

What we are saying is that the extra money *must* be found: urgently, because if it isn't, the world has no hope of achieving the Millennium Development Goals.

In 2000, all 189 member states of the United Nations agreed eight measures aimed at halving world poverty by 2015: read the next page with care – because these are important. These are promises, actual promises that we made.

The Millennium Development Goals –

to be achieved by 2015

1. Tackling extreme poverty – halving the number of people living on less than $1 a day.

2. Achieving universal primary education – ensuring all boys and girls complete primary schooling.

3. Promoting gender equality – making sure there are the same numbers of boys and girls in primary and secondary education, preferably by 2005.

4. Reducing child mortality – cutting the death rate among children under five by two-thirds.

5. Improving maternal health – reducing maternal deaths by three-quarters.

6. Combating HIV/AIDS, malaria and other diseases.

7. Ensuring environmental sustainability – reducing by half the number of people without access to safe drinking water and basic sanitation; reversing the loss of environmental resources and significantly improving the lives of 100 million slum-dwellers.

8. Developing a global partnership for development – working together on debt, trade, public health, aid and technology issues to promote economic growth and poverty reduction.

Our government made these promises. We must make sure they stick to them . . .

Some people are now saying these goals were just a dream – that they're too tough for the world to deliver. But what exactly are our priorities? Here are a few statistics that put these things into perspective:

Universal primary education – every child just getting basic schooling – **would cost $10 billion a year, less than the US spends on ice cream.**

Reproductive health services for *all* women – making childbirth safer – **would cost $12 billion a year, which is what we currently spend on perfume in Europe and the US.**

Basic healthcare and nutrition would cost $13 billion a year. **Europe and the US currently spend $17 billion a year on pet food.**

At current rates of progress on just one of the Millennium Development Goals – primary education for all – **Kylie Minogue will be 162 years old when the target is reached.**

And by the time we've stopped the completely unnecessary deaths of under-fives, **Justin Timberlake will be 184.**

And

actually works!

Well, of course, the spending of money will always be complicated. But in many of the poorest countries, private investment is simply not an option: armed conflict, lack of infrastructure and an untrained workforce make it impossible to attract business. Aid is the only realistic option for investment – but the good thing about aid is that it can be directly targeted at reducing poverty. It does actually work.

In 2002, Tanzania made primary education free and compulsory. Debt relief made this possible initially, but then it was aid that built the necessary extra classrooms. As a result, 1.6 million more children now attend school.

Thanks to aid, Ugandans no longer have to pay for basic healthcare (which many people cannot afford) and attendance at health clinics has doubled, as has child immunization against avoidable, life-threatening diseases..

Road improvements in Ethiopia financed by aid have enabled more children to get to school, have cut down the time it takes to collect water and fuel, and have reduced costs to farmers of taking their goods to market.

Aid to isolated groups of indigenous people in Bolivia has allowed them to serve in local governments for the first time and given women a voice in how their lives are run.

The To Do List: 3

Wear a white band.

The white band is the symbol of the Make Poverty History campaign: wearing it during 2005 will send a message that you want poverty to be stopped. It will tell people that you want to see action on debt, trade and aid. The band can be worn any way you like: on your wrist, on your arm, in your hair, through the laces in your trainers, around your rear-view mirror, through the straps in your handbag, as a lapel ribbon, on your key ring, even on pet collars.

How to get a white band:

* Online
* On the high street
* On the phone
* By SMS
* By post

Online:
From **ActionAid, Christian Aid/Traidcraft, EveryChild, Oxfam, Save the Children,** or **World Vision**

On the High Street:
Oxfam, Save the Children and Body Shop

By SMS:
Through **Oxfam**: text BAND to 87140 (cost of text £1.50 for the initial message, plus your standard text rates. Cost includes p&p)

On the phone:
Action Aid – 01460 238027
Christian Aid – 08700 787 788
EveryChild – 020 7749 2490
Save the Children – 020 7012 6400
World Vision – 0870 850 2005
World Development Movement – 020 7738 3311

By post:
– See the Make Poverty History website for latest stock details

ActionAid
Chataway House
Leach Road
Chard
Somerset
TA20 1FR
(cotton or silicon bands for £1, or handwoven bands from Bangladesh for £1.50. Cheques to ActionAid, with your full postal address)

EveryChild
4 Bath Place
Rivington St
London EC2A 3DR

Christian Aid
PO Box 30
Alton
GU34 4PY
(cotton and silicon bands, both £1 each. Cheques to Christian Aid Ltd, with your full postal address and how many bands of each type you'd like to order)

World Development Movement
25 Beehive Place
London SW9 7QR
(cotton band for £1. Cheques to World Development Movement, with your full postal address)

Plus: Ask everyone you know if they will be able to make it to Edinburgh on 2 July. (See To Do List: 7 on page 60.) Get anyone who can't go to send their message – preferably on white cloth for maximum impact – with someone who is going.

> *I am proud to wear the symbol of this Global Call To Action in 2005. This white band is from my country. In a moment, I want to give this band to you – young people of Britain – and ask you to take it forward along with millions of others to the G8 summit in July. I entrust it to you. I will be watching with anticipation.*

Nelson Mandela

'All of the incessant debate about development assistance, and whether the rich are doing enough to help the poor, actually concerns less than 1% of rich world income. The effort required of the rich is indeed so slight that to do less is to announce brazenly to a large part of the world: "You count for nothing." We should not be surprised, then, if in later years the rich reap the whirlwind of that heartless response.'

Jeffrey Sachs, special adviser to UN General Secretary Kofi Annan on the Millennium Development Goals

Not so amusing facts . . .

◼ If the UK met the target of 0.7% of national income in aid by 2008, an extra 1.5 million people could beat poverty that year.

◼ The UK and Spain have set themselves targets to reach the 0.7% goal. But most countries still have no timetable. At current rates of progress, Canada won't reach the target until 2025, the USA won't reach it until 2040 and Germany won't get there till 2087.

◼ For rich countries, the 0.7% goal is the equivalent of half the money we currently spend subsidizing our own farmers.

This is not about charity, it's about justice. And that's too bad. Because you're good at charity. The British, like the Irish, are good at it. Even the poorest neighbourhoods give more than they can afford. We like to give, and we give a lot. But justice is a tougher standard. Africa makes a fool of our idea of justice; it makes a farce of our idea of equality. It mocks our pieties, it doubts our concern, it questions our commitment. Because there's no way we can look at Africa – a continent bursting into flames – and if we're honest conclude that it would ever be allowed to happen anywhere else . . .

"The war against terror is bound up in the war against poverty" – I didn't say that, Colin Powell said that . . . In these disturbing and distressing times, surely it's cheaper, and smarter, to make friends out of potential enemies than it is to defend yourself against them.

Africa is not the frontline of the war against terror. But it could be soon. Justice is the surest way to get peace.

Bono

Labour Party Conference, September 2004

Step 4

Get to Grips with Trade Justice

If you did get stuck in that very unreliable lift with the Prime Minister, do you think you could mutter something about 'trade justice' but wouldn't want to let the conversation go much further because you've no idea what it actually is?

Don't worry. It is possible to understand trade justice without a PhD in economics. Just listen to Solomon Mbewe, who, with his wife Joyce, is a cotton farmer in Zambia . . .

The cotton that Solomon and Joyce grow pays for schooling for their five children, for clothes, for the food they cannot grow, and for other necessities, such as oil and salt – and last year, they were hoping, also for some corrugated iron to roof the small hut where they and their children live.

It didn't happen. The price they got for their cotton in 2004 was so low that they only made enough to repay the costs of the seeds and the fertilizer. 'I failed,' Solomon says, 'in my vision of getting a better roof.'

Cotton farmers like Solomon and Joyce have suffered from low prices since the early 1990s, when the World Bank and the International Monetary Fund (IMF) forced Zambia to open up to cotton imports, driving down the price local farmers could get for their own cotton. At the same time, Zambia was also expected to cut financial support that it gave to Solomon and Joyce and their fellow cotton farmers.

The United States meanwhile paid its own cotton farmers $3.9 billion in subsidies in 2000/2001 – three times more than its entire aid budget for Africa's 800 million people.

By 2001 America's cotton had captured 41% of the world market, driving down prices everywhere. That's all you need to know, really: poor countries, already economically disadvantaged by destitution (bad roads, few trucks, not enough power generators or irrigation channels, depleted soil), are further disadvantaged by trade rules written by the rich. These too often force them to cut support to their own farmers and traders and allow developed countries to dump cheap exports on them.

The rich countries call it free trade, but what is free about having your hands tied by poverty?

During the 1980s and the 1990s, the International Monetary Fund and the World Bank virtually ran the economic policies of Africa.

In return for giving aid and a measure of debt relief, these international institutions forced poor countries to slash their spending, often on crucial basic services. But by the start of the twenty-first century, the poorest countries are poorer than they were in the 1960s, when the World Bank first arrived on the scene.

Clearly, something isn't working.

Before you finish eating your breakfast this morning, you've depended on half the world. This is the way our universe is structured . . . We aren't going to have peace on earth until we recognize this basic fact.

Martin Luther King

In 2003, for example, the Ghanaian government decided to protect its rice growers from imports of (often subsidized) rice from elsewhere, including the United States. Within days, the IMF had forced Ghana to back down: its rice farmers could not, after all, be protected.

The World Bank and IMF made Ghana open up its agricultural markets. The end result has been that the US now provides 40% of Ghana's rice imports. Ghana's own production has collapsed – local rice farmers in Ghana can no longer make a living. And in countries like Ghana, most people are farmers.

The rich world repeatedly uses its financial muscle to boss the poor world around, allegedly for its own good, but too often it seems that the people who really benefit are the rich.

Our country, along with other developed nations, likes to preach free trade and self-help, even while we make self-help more difficult.

Rich countries need to live up to what they say. They need to stop forcing free trade on the poor in the belief that it's *always* a good thing for everyone. Poor countries must have the right to support their farmers, traders and industries.

Do you think it's right

that a poor country like Tanzania is forced to privatize its utilities, with the result that its water system is now owned and run by a UK multinational? Particularly when this multinational is now supplying water that many people can't afford! The poorest people of Tanzania are still having to use water from shallow local wells, which is often dirty and makes them sick.

Do you think it's right

that around half of the European Union's annual budget is spent on the Common Agricultural Policy, producing more food than we need, surpluses of things like sugar, for example, which then drive down world prices? Or that this then destroys the livelihoods of farmers in poor countries? Or that the EU then dumps its surpluses on those countries?

Do you think it's right

that poor countries should sometimes be forced as a condition of getting aid money from rich countries to cut government spending on health, education and subsidies for poor farmers (yes, actually forced to cut them!)?

Let's say you think all those things are wrong – what do you argue when someone protests that the World Bank and the IMF were set up to help the developing world and that one way and another they give loads of money to poor countries?

You could point out that they're dominated by the rich world, so that the needs of the developing countries are often not heard. Or you could just tell them about Benta.

Benta's story: part one

Benta, a widow, lives in the Nyando district of Kenya and struggles to support her five children, aged between five and seventeen, on the money she earns by labouring on other people's sugar cane farms.

Since 2000, when Kenya lifted restrictions on sugar imports, the local market has been flooded with cheap imports. As a result, sugar-processing factories have shut, workers been laid off and farmers brought close to bankruptcy. Wages have fallen sharply: Benta used to earn 33p for weeding one row of sugar cane; now she gets 24p. Here in the UK people usually expect to get paid more as the years go by – it's the opposite for Benta. In a good week, Benta earns £2, with which she buys milk, maize, soap, sugar, cooking fat and matchsticks. Since the household lost her husband's income, she has found it difficult to make enough money for the most basic needs of her family. He died a few years ago, probably, she thinks, of AIDS. Benta now suspects that she and her five-year-old daughter may also be HIV positive.

'Before, I could weed two rows of sugar cane in a day. But now I can only do one row in a day and mostly I can't finish it. I get very tired nowadays. I think I get tired because of the disease I suspect I have, but mainly because I'm poor. I don't have much to eat to get the energy I need for weeding.'

Free trade is making Benta poorer.

'I was wrong. Free market trade policies hurt the poor . . . the rules of international trade are rigged against the poorest countries.'

Stephen Byers, former Secretary of State for Trade and Industry

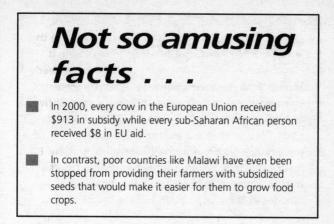

Not so amusing facts . . .

- In 2000, every cow in the European Union received $913 in subsidy while every sub-Saharan African person received $8 in EU aid.

- In contrast, poor countries like Malawi have even been stopped from providing their farmers with subsidized seeds that would make it easier for them to grow food crops.

'International trade between my country and the West is like an antelope and a giraffe competing for food which is at the top of a tree. You can make the ground beneath their feet level, but the contest will still not be fair.'

Dr Robert Aboagye-Mensah, General Secretary, Christian Council of Ghana

'Trade's a fundamental issue, and if we don't bring it on the agenda now, it's never going to get on the agenda.'

Thom Yorke, Radiohead

The To Do List: 4

Vote for trade justice. This is a scheme to register as many votes as possible – certainly at least a million by the time of the World Trade Organization meeting in Hong Kong in December – to prove to politicians that trade justice matters. When a similar vote was held in Brazil, a huge number of people – 8 million – registered their opposition to free trade.

You can vote online at the Make Poverty History website or at www.tjm.org.uk or you can text JUSTICE to 84118 (at your operator's standard rate).

Your vote will send the message to politicians that they should

* insist that governments, particularly in poor countries, should choose their own best solutions to end poverty and protect the environment.

* stop the dumping of exports that damage the lives of poor people around the world.

* make laws to stop big business profiting at the expense of people and the environment.

Time taken: 10 minutes at most.
Cost: none.

Step 5

Let's Finish Off This Debt Thing Once and for All

You've heard the stories about unscrupulous moneylenders offering loans to poor people at extortionate rates that only drive them deeper into debt. That's pretty much what we're doing to poor countries.

Perhaps you supported the Jubilee 2000 campaign. Perhaps you were even one of the 70,000 people surrounding the G8 summit in Birmingham in 1998, protesting that you were no longer prepared to see £3 siphoned off in debt repayment from poor countries for every £1 we give in aid.

Even if you're too young to remember much about that, you probably know that, largely as a result of the Jubilee campaign, the UK has unilaterally cancelled 100% of the debt directly owed to it by the world's poorest countries. We've also agreed to write off our share of the debts the poorest countries owed to Britain indirectly through the World Bank and the African Development Bank.

This is a real success story, and we can feel proud that the UK has taken a lead. But globally, unfortunately, little more than 10% of the debt owed by the poorest countries to the richest has been cancelled.

Debt cancellation is the great unfinished business of the twentieth century.

Malawi spends more on servicing debt than on healthcare, even though one in five Malawians is HIV positive.

Zambia pays $25 million a year to the IMF, although 40% of rural women are unable to read and write.

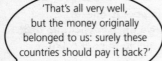

Q: 'That's all very well, but the money originally belonged to us: surely these countries should pay it back?'

A: 'We in the rich world have to take responsibility for the debt crisis too. We lent irresponsibly to their governments and we've driven poor countries into a cul-de-sac. And it's their poorest people, not their governments, that are paying the price – where are they supposed to turn to for help? In fact, it's not only unfair to insist that they repay, it's not even in our interest. Look at what happened after the First World War, when crippling demands for Germany to pay back money contributed to the rise of the Nazis. Or after the Second World War, when the opposite happened and America pumped money back into Europe with the Marshall Plan, helping to restore social and economic order.'

In our own time, too, there's ample evidence that debt relief works:

'In 2001, Tanzania was granted significant debt relief. As promised, this was directed to the priority sectors of education, health, water, rural roads and HIV/AIDS.

Now the primary school population has increased by 66%; we have built 45,000 classrooms and 1,925 primary schools; we have recruited 37,261 new teachers between 2000 and 2004, and retrained another 14,852. At this rate, we believe that the goal of universal basic education can be attained in 2006, nine years ahead of the 2015 target! . . . Tanzania has shown dramatic improvements after getting partial debt relief. Clearly, much more can be done with total debt cancellation.'

Benjamin William Mkapa, president of the United Republic of Tanzania

Not so amusing facts . . .

■ One-third of deaths – some 18 million people per year or 50,000 per day – are due to poverty-related causes. That's 270 million people since 1990, the majority women and children, roughly equal to the population of the US.

■ Nigeria borrowed $5 billion, has paid $16 billion to date and still owes $32 billion.

So debt relief can be hugely effective, but is it really necessary to have all three – debt relief, trade justice, and more and better aid? Absolutely.

You'd probably like to be a bit better off. You probably aim to be a bit better off at some point in the future. And luckily for you, you live in a place where that remains a constant possibility. Not a single country in Western Europe, North America or East Asia has failed to achieve economic growth between 1980 and 2000.

But some countries never get a chance to improve themselves. Their populations are very poor – often because of unjust trade – so governments can't really raise enough taxes to fix things – there's just not enough money around. So the government can't build all the support systems – good roads, ports, telecommunications and so on – that a successful society needs. The same countries get hit hardest by disease and by climate shocks, like earthquakes and droughts. When this happens, they may be forced to seek more loans – which often come with damaging conditions attached. Paying for these debts then makes government even less able to build the infrastructure for a successful economy. And still they can't raise taxes, because the population is so poor. It's a vicious circle.

That's why Make Poverty History insists that aid, trade and debt are inextricably linked; it won't be enough to pick off one. All three have to be addressed together for poverty to be defeated, to make extreme poverty history.

Economists are always reminding us that wealth is not a zero-sum game: in other words, you are not part of the rich world because a poor world exists. Poor countries are poor because they're caught in a poverty trap. We have to find a way of integrating them into the world economy. Which will eventually be better for everyone. By making everyone richer, we also make everyone safer.

'The rich do not have to invest enough in the poorest countries to make them rich; they need to invest enough so that these countries can get their foot on the economic ladder . . . Economic development works. It can be successful. It tends to build on itself. But it must get started.'

Jeffrey Sachs

Not so amusing facts . . .

- Each year, 17 million people die of diseases that we know how to cure.

- It is estimated that if the price of the ten most important tropical commodities, such as cocoa, sugar and cotton, had risen with inflation, the countries that produce these goods would have earned almost five times the total world annual aid budget in 2002.

- 20% of aid promised by the European Union arrives more than a year late – a year in which 11 million children will die unnecessarily.

The To Do List: 5

Join a campaigning group

Make Poverty History is not one organization – it's about 400. Each of those organizations is working to help overcome poverty and injustice and will go on working until the job is done. They all need your help. You can make a difference by offering your support. Maybe you want to meet other supporters who live near you and share your passion for changing the world. Maybe you want to join an organization that matches your interests – as a student, a pensioner, a trade unionist, a professional, a member of a particular faith . . . Perhaps you want to support an organization that's working directly in some of the poorest countries. Or you might want to throw your weight behind a small organization that you've never heard of – but looks like it's got the right idea!

All the organizations are listed at www.makepovertyhistory.org.

Follow the links. Sign up. Volunteer. Get involved.

Step 6

Be Absolutely Certain – Poverty Kills

Don't doubt for one minute that lives are at stake here. Benta's story below is a classic example of how poverty kills: poverty is causing AIDS, and AIDS has already killed 24 million people in sub-Saharan Africa. In rich countries, drugs are available that reverse the progess of HIV and keep people alive and healthy for up to twenty years. But in Africa, with medicines out of reach of the poor, HIV is still a death sentence.

Poverty is the key – the developing countries have 95% of the AIDS cases worldwide. And if anyone asks why, if these people are already so poor, they don't help themselves by practising safe sex – well, poverty itself is the answer. Read on.

Benta's story: part two

We left Benta, the sugar cane labourer from the Nyando district of Kenya, on page 38, suspecting that she and her five-year-old daughter might be HIV positive. 'I'm not sure I'm positive,' she says, 'but I know what I'm feeling. I know I'm not healthy. And my daughter has never been healthy like my other children.'

Despite her worries, Benta has decided not to have an HIV test.

'I would have wished to confirm my status, but when I thought of the poverty I'm in and what I could do with the money, I chose to ignore the test.'

The test wouldn't cost anything, but Benta would have to give up a day's work to travel to the health centre. She can't afford the loss of income. Besides, it's not clear what good it would do her to know: the antiretroviral drugs that would help her control her HIV have come down in price from £48 to £6.90 a month (thanks to international campaigning). But they're still way beyond her budget.

She's already sold what assets she had: 'I sold all my livestock – two cows, and all my sheep and goats – to pay for healthcare for my husband when he was sick.'

So if Benta is HIV positive, sooner or later she will develop AIDS and, because she can't afford treatment, she will die. She doesn't want to talk about what will happen then to her children. So far, she's been able to keep them at school; but in many other families, children, especially girls, are taken out of school to care for sick relatives, or to work, or simply because their parents can no longer afford uniforms or books.

But this is another part of the vicious circle.
For young people who have completed primary education are less than half as likely to contract HIV. Education is one of the best weapons the world has against AIDS.

It's also doubtful whether Benta's relatives will be able to support any more hungry people if Benta dies. In the past, grandparents, uncles and aunts would automatically have taken care of orphans, but poverty is now so great (and the number of orphans so high) that they can't afford to do so. Increasing numbers of households are headed by children; there are more and more street children, without adult support, who will do anything for food.

'There is much, much more HIV than five years ago,' Benta says, 'because many parents are dead, and since they were the breadwinners the families left behind are in absolute poverty. So this makes the youth get involved in sexual practices to support their siblings.

'I believe it is the drop in the [sugar cane] price and the closure of the industry that has made people very poor and desperate. And that has led them to indulge in indiscriminate sexual practices.'

'HIV is one of the greatest threats to eradicating poverty.'

UK Government report, July 2004

So poverty and AIDS
create a downward spiral:

Poverty

▼

The need to earn money forces people into dangerous sexual behaviour

▼

AIDS leaves children without parents, schools without teachers, and companies and governments without skilled workers

▼

Education suffers – and the unskilled and illiterate are more vulnerable to HIV infection (especially women)

▼

The economy suffers – and there's less money to invest in healthcare and development

▼

People are so desperate that treating HIV infection seems less urgent than eating

▼

There's more migration, especially to urban centres where there's a market for commercial sex

▼

People who are HIV positive see no point in investing in the future

▼

Social structures break down

↙ ↘

Increasing opportunities to trade sex   **Economic breakdown**

Most illnesses strike the very young and very old, with horrible consequences. But HIV/AIDS is killing adults in their prime. As a result, around 12 million children in Africa have lost one or both parents.

In the hardest-hit countries of Southern Africa, one in three adults is HIV positive.

It's not difficult to imagine what sort of an impact this would have on any society – let alone one that was already barely surviving. But if you want facts and figures, the World Bank has estimated that after twenty years some countries will be 67% worse off than they would have been without HIV.

The short-term effects are bad enough (a study in Zambia suggested that most households that had lost their breadwinner to HIV experienced a massive 80% drop in income) but the long-term implications are frightening too. No one is bringing up or teaching the children – as the World Bank itself has noted:

'HIV causes far greater long-term damage to economies than previously assumed, for by killing mostly young adults, the disease is robbing the children of AIDS victims of one or both parents to love, raise and educate them, and so undermines the basis of economic growth over the long haul.'

Not so amusing facts . . .

- Over 3 million people died from AIDS in 2004. 2.3 million of those were in sub-Saharan Africa. That amounts to 8,493 people dying from AIDS every day and six people dying every minute.

- Aid to the 28 countries with the highest HIV adult prevalence rate declined by one-third between 1995 and 2000.

- A World Bank study has concluded that, unless further action is taken, current rates of HIV in South Africa will result in complete economic collapse within three generations.

The To Do List: 6

E-lobby politicians to Stop AIDS

Go to the Stop AIDS campaign website **www.stopaidscampaign.org.uk** and take the e-action asking politicians to commit to provide HIV treatment to all those that need it. The action is being updated throughout 2005 so that it always targets the right key decision-makers.

Time taken: 5 minutes.
Cost: none.

Earlier I described the deaths of 6,500 Africans a day from a preventable treatable disease like AIDS: I watched people queueing up to die, three in a bed in Malawi. That's Africa's crisis.

But the fact that we in Europe or America are not treating it like an emergency – and the fact that it's not every day on the news, well that is our crisis . . .

This is not about "doing our best". It's win or lose. Life or death. Literally so.

We are the first generation that can look extreme and stupid poverty in the eye, look across the water to Africa and elsewhere, and say this and mean it: we have the cash, we have the drugs, we have the science – but do we have the will?

Do we have the will to make poverty history?

Bono

Labour Party Conference, September 2004

Step 7

Get Your Questions Answered

OK, so everyone agrees that it's a good thing to end extreme poverty, disease and despair. No one would admit to being politically _against_ it. And since we agree that we know how to do it, it's incredible it isn't happening.

One problem is that there remain misconceptions. How, for example, do you answer people who claim that the poor countries will never recover as long as their leaders are corrupt? Or that more aid is only going to result in more hungry mouths to feed? Or that Africans have fallen behind in the world economy because, basically, they're lazy?

Here are some possible answers to some of those questions:

Q: _If we gave more money to poor countries, wouldn't it just disappear into the pockets of corrupt leaders?_

A: There's no doubt that there has been, and still is, corruption in poor countries.

Unfortunately, poverty and bad government create and sustain each other. (Yes, it's another vicious circle.) This means that turning our backs on the people of badly run poor countries will only make matters worse.

To get good government, people need space to think about something other than the next meal. They need sufficient education to read books and newspapers; they need access to television, telephones and the internet so that they can spread ideas, organize opposition, campaign and create democracy.

They need a proper civil service to keep politicians in line, to establish rules and monitor them. They need to earn enough to pay taxes, to provide computers and staff and all the other tools of a modern state.

The levels of corruption we have seen in very poor countries couldn't happen here because our democratic state would root them out: angry people would protest, vote, insist on legal action. But you can't get democracy and law without basic levels of well-being and prosperity. And without democracy and law, it's difficult for people to better themselves.

There is a long history of corruption in Western countries too. We're also not exactly innocent when it comes to exploiting poor nations. And the developed world has been known to shut its eyes to bribery. This isn't something in 'national character': power corrupts if it isn't constantly kept in check. So the route to better government doesn't lie in making life even tougher for poor people, punishing those who are already at a disadvantage. The route to better government lies in helping people to find, create and seize the tools they need to control their own destinies.

Not giving aid because there have been examples of corruption would be like closing down all companies because Enron cheated.

'There is no evidence whatsoever that Africa is poorly governed by the standards of very poor countries.'

Jeffrey Sachs, special adviser to UN General Secretary Kofi Annan on the Millennium Development Goals

'I went to Johannesburg recently for a meeting of leaders of this campaign from forty countries. There was a lot of talk there of making sure that aid gets through to the right people. Interestingly, it was the representatives from Africa and the poorest countries who were most passionate about forcing their governments to clean up their act.

Everything must be done to create good governance so that aid works. That will be part of the solution. This is not the time to say: "It's very tricky, so let's walk away."'

Richard Curtis

Q: *Aren't poor people lazy/ Don't they lack modern values/ Aren't they unpunctual/ Aren't they just not individualistic in the way that people in the West are?*

A: It so happens that there's a long history of misunderstanding of the people of less developed countries. (It's enormously comforting to assume you're doing better because you're smarter rather than because you're luckier.) Early Western visitors to Japan wrote home of the people's 'love of indolence' and suggested Western ways of doing things would never work because of native 'weediness and corruption'.

In the early twentieth century the Catholic societies of Italy and Ireland were thought by many to be incapable of economic growth, on account of their supposed superstitiousness and lack of moral fibre.

India's poverty was widely believed to be the consequence of Hindu mysticism and social rigidities until India became one of the fastest-growing economies of the world in the 1990s.

When social scientists try to measure attitudes to work, child rearing and education, though, the stereotypes quickly collapse. The World Values Survey poses identical questions to households around the world. In 2000, people were asked whether it's especially important for children to learn 'hard work' at home. 61% of Americans said yes, compared to 80% of Nigerians, 75% of South Africans, and 83% of Tanzanians.

Q: *If we could save the lives of more children who are currently dying of poverty, won't that just lead to a population explosion and more mouths to feed?*

A: When children die in large numbers, parents tend to have more of them to provide security for the family in later years. As a result, and contrary to popular belief, places with high child-mortality rates also have high population growth. It's actually because people are poor that they have more children.

The better off that families become, and the more educated the mothers and children, the fewer children they tend to have and the more they invest in them. On the question of high population, the opposite of what people think is true.

In any event, 'population explosion' is a red herring because in most cases poor people go hungry because they can't afford to buy the food in the markets, not because the markets are empty. On top of this, many of the resources that could feed the populations of the developing world are shipped out to the rich world, including millions of tons of food (soya from South America to feed North American cattle, for example). And of course the environmental impact of each person in the rich world is much greater.

Twenty years ago, shortly after Live Aid, Bono and his wife Ali went to Ethiopia, 'on the quiet, to see for ourselves what was going on'. They lived there for a month, working at an orphanage.

Africa is a magical place. And anybody who ever gave anything there got a lot more back. A shining shining continent, with beautiful royal faces: Ethiopia not just blew my mind, it opened my mind.

On our last day at the orphanage a man handed me his baby and said: "Take him with you." He knew in Ireland his son would live; in Ethiopia his son would die.

I turned him down.

In that moment, I started this journey. In that moment, I became the worst thing of all: a rock star with a cause.

Except this isn't a cause. 6,500 Africans dying a day of treatable, preventable disease – dying for want of medicines you and I can get at our local chemist – that's not a cause, that's an emergency.

Bono

Labour Party Conference, September 2004

The To Do List: 7

Go to Edinburgh on 2 July

On 2 July you have the chance to make history, like those campaigners we started off with, who fought against slavery, apartheid and debt.

In all those cases, politicians were forced to take action by the sheer weight of numbers protesting that what had previously seemed inevitable or unstoppable was wrong and could be changed.

On 2 July the leaders of the Group of 8 (with the EU present as an observer) will begin to arrive in Scotland as the summit gets under way. The G8 conference is designed to allow them to discuss issues facing the world in an informal setting – this year, at the Gleneagles Hotel. They won't vote, but they could agree on major initiatives that would change the fate of the poorest people.

Imagine what it will be like for them to arrive in Edinburgh to find the city encircled by a human white band: hundreds of thousands of protesters wearing white, wearing their white bands, bearing messages to be delivered to them at Gleneagles. Imagine the extra pressure if every news broadcast says that issues of poverty are absolutely key – that the world demands results on debt, trade and aid.

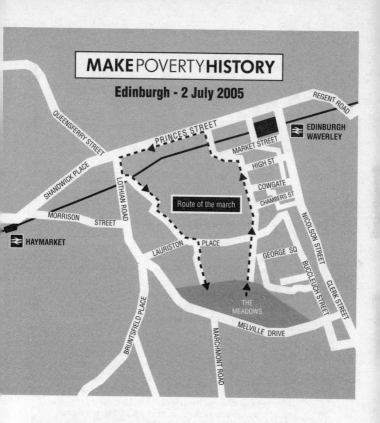

The rally will start at 11 a.m. in The Meadows, with two stages featuring speeches from international figures and celebrity supporters, and live music acts, as well as food, drink and activities all day

* A staggered march on a circular route will begin at noon and continue until 2 p.m. to create a giant human white band. Bring friends, family and children. Wear white and put all your messages on white cloth or card to maximize the impact of the human band. You'll have a chance to add your messages to a giant display, which will be delivered to the G8 leaders.

* You can download all the latest information on the day from the website www.makepovertyhistory.org.

STOP PRESS

* Just as we are printing this book it's been announced that 'Live 8' is going to happen in early July, twenty years after the first Live Aid concert. But this time it's not about charity, it's about justice – a free concert that is asking not for your money but for your voice.

* The rally in Edinburgh on 2 July will now spearhead an unprecedented burst of popular pressure to make poverty history. If you can't get to Edinburgh, you can be part of Live 8. Wherever you are that weekend – Edinburgh, Hyde Park, or at home watching the concert on television – make sure you take action and add your voice to the millions around the world who want to make poverty history.

* And when the concert is over, let's make sure those world leaders meeting in Scotland know we won't go away until they act.